HENRY PURCELL

SONATAS OF THREE PARTS

Nos. 7 – 12

Edited with a foreword by/
Herausgegeben mit einem Vorwort von
Roger Fiske

T0081310

Ernst Eulenburg Ltd

London · Mainz · Madrid · New York · Paris · Tokyo · Toronto · Zürich

© 1975 Ernst Eulenburg Ltd., London
Printed by Caligraving Ltd., Thetford, Norfolk.

HENRY PURCELL
Twelve Sonatas of Three Parts

The earliest English trio sonatas were probably those Coperario wrote in about 1620; born John Cooper, he had changed his name after a visit to Italy where no doubt he heard some of the first Italian sonatas of this kind. More interesting examples were being composed about 1640 by William Lawes; these were in three movements called Fantasia, Alman, and Galliard,[1] and this is an indication of their likeness to the earlier fantasias and dances for viols alone. Indeed the three-part fantasia for viols became a trio sonata movement if a keyboard instrument doubled on the bass line. At this period it is often hard to tell if a composer wanted a keyboard instrument or not. When Matthew Locke published his *Little Consort* in 1656 he apparently did not mind which way the suites for 'two trebles and a bass' were played, for the title-page specifically says: 'To be performed either alone or with theorbo's and harpsecord'. Further more he apparently did not mind if the 'trebles' were viols or violins.

About this time John Jenkins was composing chamber works that bear a somewhat closer resemblance to the Baroque trio sonata. They are musically more substantial than Locke's *Little Consort* (each suite consisted of four short dance-movements), and they positively demand violins for the 'treble' parts and a keyboard instrument to fill in the harmonies from the bass line. The more incisive tone of the violin was especially needed in the quicker movements in which an element of virtuosity was beginning to appear; the development of the violin in Italy was making possible a quite new style of playing for which composers were beginning to provide. Nevertheless in England the bass viol continued to be preferred to the cello until after Purcell's death, while the keyboard instrument was as likely to be an organ as a harpsichord; many people had chamber organs in their homes. A number of Jenkins' trio sonatas survive in MS, and some are said to have been published in 1660; Purcell certainly knew them.

Purcell's trio sonatas differ from those of his English predecessors in two main respects; first, they are much more interesting, and secondly they are much more Italianate, especially in the quicker movements. Very few Italian trio sonatas had been published by 1683, and there is no evidence that any published examples had as yet reached England, but Italian

[1]*Musica Britannica* XXI pp. 107-126 gives three of the eight that survive, and there are examples by Coperario in *Musica Britannica* IX pp. 183-191.

musicians were beginning to arrive in London to earn their living, and they sometimes brought with them MS trio sonatas by such composers as Vitali; a British Museum MS of such sonatas, Add. 31431, is dated 1680. Purcell took a pride in the increased Italian element in his own specimens. as is stressed in the address 'To the Reader'. Significantly he has no named dances. Nevertheless the influence of the old Fantasias is still apparent in some of the movements.

On 28 May 1683 the *London Gazette* announced. 'These are to give Notice to all Gentlemen that have subscribed to the Proposals Published by Mr Henry Purcel for the Printing his Sonata's of three Parts for two Violins and Base to the Harpsicord or Organ. That the said Books are now compleatly finished, and shall be delivered to them upon the 11th of June next: And if any who have not yet Subscribed, shall before that time Subscribe, according to the said Proposals, (which is Ten Shillings the whole Sett) which are at Mr William Hall's house in Norfolk-street, or at Mr Playford's and Mr Carr's Shops in the Temple; for the said Books will not after that time be sold under 15s, the Sett.' A further announcement on 11 June invited subscribers to bring their receipts to Purcell's house 'in St Anns Lane, beyond Westminster-Abby', where they would 'receive their Books' paying the remaining part of the Money. The title-page ran as follows:

Sonnata's
of III Parts:
Two Viollins And Basse:
To the Organ or Harpsecord.
Composed By
Henry Purcell, Composer
in Ordinary to his most Sacred
Majesty, and Organist of his
Chappell Royall.
London.
Printed for the Author:
And Sold by I. Playford and I. Carr
at the Temple, Fleet Street, 1683.

Subscribers received not three but four part books, and they were labelled Violin Primo, Violin Secundo, Basso, and Basso Continuo. Only the Violin Primo has the introductory matter. This begins with a portrait of the composer in his twenty-fourth year, said to be by R. White. After the title-page described above, there is the Dedication and the address 'To the Reader' given on pages XI and XII, a repeat of the title-page, and then the music. Each sonata occupies two facing pages in each part; no turning-over is needed. By later standards the pages are small.

Critics have sometimes been puzzled that Purcell should have called these works 'Sonnata's of III Parts', and the similar ones published posthumously 'Sonatas in IV Parts', but there is no problem here. All trio sonatas need four players, but usually the same part serves for the bass viol and the keyboard player. Purcell's publisher may well have expected the basso part to be of this kind, and he had his title-page engraved accordingly. The address 'To the Reader' says that the composer had second thoughts on this subject, but, as we shall see later, Purcell must always have wanted four part books; when he insisted on four, Playford refused to go to the expense of correcting the title-page. It seems likely that the address 'To the Reader' was written not by Purcell but by Playford.

The unusual accuracy of the part-books testifies to the care with which Purcell proof-read them, and this is mentioned in the address 'To the Reader'. No autograph survives for these sonatas, but even if it did the published parts would take preference as representing the composer's final thoughts. The text of this edition is therefore that of the published parts. The two sets consulted for this score differ very occasionally as regards slurs, accidentals, and continuo figures; no doubt further variants could be found in sets elsewhere. A full collation has not been attempted, but a few of the differences are mentioned in the Textual Notes.

Four seventeenth century MS scores survive. The beautiful one in the library of Christ Church College, Oxford (MS 39) shows every sign of having been made from the set of published parts which this library also possesses, and it is therefore of little value editorially. Of much more interest is RM MS 20.h.9 at the British Museum, which diverges from the published parts in a number of particulars; the words at the top of the first page, 'Aged 25 in the years 1683', conflict with the date of Purcell's birth as generally accepted today. W. H. Cummings once owned a score which he believed, incorrectly, was in Purcell's hand, and it was accepted as the autograph by J. A. Fuller-Maitland, who listed the main points in which it differed from the published parts in his Purcell Society edition of 1893; the MS is now in the Eastman School of Music, Rochester, N.Y. (Sibley 151841). There is yet another score in the Conservatoire Royal de Musique, Brussels (MS V. 14.981).

The first eight sonatas are in pairs, a sonata in the minor key being followed by one in the relative major. These pairs move stepwise from flat keys to sharp ones. The last four sonatas break this pattern, but it may be significant that the first two works in the later *Sonatas of IV Parts* are in the keys required to preserve the pattern, B minor and E flat. Originally the E flat may have been paired with the C minor standing at No. IX in the 1683 set, and the B minor with the D Major (XII) at the end. Furthermore, there are stylistic reasons for suspecting that the B minor and E flat of the second set may originally have belonged to the first set. The opening Adagio of the former and the second Adagio of the latter begin with a repeated-note theme in dotted rhythm, the repeated notes being a fifth above the tonic. No other slow movements start in this way in the second set, but a surprising number do so in the 1683 set; see for instance I 67, V 101, VII 100, VIII 125, X 88, and XI 1; see also IX 117.

Other movements also fall into families. Thus the fugue towards the middle of each sonata is especially Italianate; when, as is usual, it is in common time, it is normally labelled Canzona and perhaps was always so labelled in the last autograph. Often there is another fugal movement towards the end of each sonata, and this has a more dancing rhythm than the Canzonas. Fugal devices include inversion (XII 105-109) and canon by augmentation (X 124). Ingenious examples of the latter occur in the opening section of VI, a canon in two-fold augmentation at the fifth and the octave. It will be noticed that these fugal movements do not treat a succession of subjects as in the old fantasias, but are restricted to the tune or tunes at the start.

The Basso Continuo notes at the beginning of these fugal movements are almost certainly cues showing the keyboard player where to come in. Such passages are nearly always a short-hand version of the violin parts, and in this score they appear in small notes (with the addition of editorial rests) because I believe they should not be played. However there are places where the 'cue' briefly provides an independent bass (III 149, IV 25-6, VII 31-2, IX 83), the implications of such passages are not clear.

It is also curious that occasional notes in the 'cues' should be figured.

The Basso and Basso Continuo parts sometimes enjoy an unusual independence (II 1-10, V 129, VI 79-82 and 149-150, IX 3-16, and XI 30). In the *Largo* from V they are independent throughout. Perhaps Purcell borrowed this movement from something he had written for four-part string band, and the question arises as to whether an additional stringed instrument is needed here to double the keyboard bass. Such passages must have been in Purcell's mind when he insisted on a separate Basso Continuo part; without one, the music would make no sense.

EDITORIAL PROCEDURE

I have cut 'Sonnata' (or 'Sonnatta') and 'A 3' in the title of each work. Purcell's clefs needed no modernizing except in the Basso Continuo 'cues', most of which were originally given in the soprano clef. I have changed three brief passages in the Basso and Basso Continuo parts from the alto to the bass clef (V 125-6, IX 91, X 22-3). I have kept all Purcell's time signatures except the $\frac{6}{4}$ in IX 130. The only other one that does not accord with modern practice is $C\atop3$ which usually means $\frac{3}{2}$ but can also mean $\frac{3}{4}$ (XI 69). I have not thought it necessary to list a variant, $C\atop31$, which sometimes occurs in one of the four parts, and never in more than two. Purcell's double barlines have been kept without additions; those in the middle of a movement imply repeats (VI 109). When a tempo change or dynamic change occurs in mid-bar, Purcell usually put a small diagonal stroke in one of the parts to show precisely where the change should occur (I 79 and X 135); these too have been kept without addition. I have changed tied minims into semibreves, and modernized the way of tying notes across a barline. All editorial additions are in brackets (there are very few), except for editorial ties and slurs which have a vertical stroke through the middle. All editorial slurs are justified by authentic slurs in similar passages elsewhere.

Pause marks at the ends of movements are puzzlingly inconsistent. One would expect that Purcell would write a pause only above the top stave, and that his engraver would sometimes forget to add it to the lower parts, but in fact Violin I has no pause marks at all except in VII 113 and in the final bar of each sonata; often it is the only part without one. Perhaps these pauses told the players of the lower staves to watch the first violin in order to get a clean start to the next section. When only one part has a pause, I have treated it as an aberration and confined it to the textual notes; when there are pauses in at least two of the parts, I have added editorial pauses in the remainder.

Purcell hardly ever presumed, as we do, that an accidental also applies to the same note later in the same bar; if he did not repeat the accidental, it was because he did not want it. Like all composers of his time he cancelled accidentals in the key signature, not with our natural sign, but with a sharp or a flat. Thus in I 42, VI. I, he wrote

If there were no sharp before note 5, one would assume an E flat. I have modernized Purcell's accidentals, cutting any that seem superfluous today and adding in brackets those a modern musician would expect (e.g. II 10 Basso). It must be stressed that bracketed naturals do not result from an editor's whim; they show what Purcell quite certainly wanted. Anyone who thinks it necessary can easily deduce Purcell's own accidentals from the above statements.

I have also cut superfluous accidentals in Purcell's key signatures, as will be clear from the above music example. I have left his two-flat key signature for Sonata IX in C minor, and his three-flat key signature for Sonata XI in F minor, because this was the usual way of writing in these keys not only in Purcell's day but in Handel's as well, but at the risk of seeming inconsistent I have adjusted his two-sharp key signature in Sonata X in A major because it was peculiar in his day and would be very confusing in ours. This change caused a good deal of adjustment in the figured bass. Here too accidentals have been modernized. It will be noticed that where there are two figures for one chord Purcell sometimes put the lower one at the top; his purpose can usually be deduced from the violin parts.

Roger Fiske, 1974

TEXTUAL NOTES

PP: Published Parts of 1683
RM: Royal Music MS 20.h.9, British Museum
S: Sibley MS 151841, Eastman School of Music
n5: the fifth note in the bar

VII	31–2	BC:	The 'cue' is an independent bass from n4 onwards
	37	Vl. I:	n1–2 slurred in **RM**; cf. Vl. II 31, etc
	44	BC:	The semibreve was given so small a space that the engraver could not show which figures went with which beat. As sometimes elsewhere, I have adjusted the figures laterally
	79		Double barline in **PP**, etc; because it implies repeats, dots have been added before and after it
	95	BC:	**PP** has *Piano* on 3rd beat of 94
	96	BC:	minim + crotchet in **PP**, etc; presumably a mistake for crotchet + minim as in **B**
	114	Vl. I:	*Vivace* in **PP**, as also for Basso; Vl. II and BC are marked *Allegro*. **RM** has *Vivace* only
	182		C (unbarred) in **RM**
VIII	45	Vl. II:	n1 F natural? (cf. Vl. I's C natural in 37) If so, perhaps **B** and BC n1 in 41 should be F natural
	51	Vl. II:	n4 C natural in **RM** and **S**, as also in BM **PP**, but C sharp in Christ Church **PP**
	76	Vl. I:	n4 should perhaps be C sharp
	90	BC:	Perhaps the dot should be replaced by a minim rest, as in **B**
	93	Vl. II:	No accidental before n5 implies F sharp, but perhaps F natural was intended
	96	Vl. II:	No accidental before n2 implies F sharp, but perhaps F natural was intended
	134	B:	*Allegro* in **PP**
IX	33	Vl. II:	**PP** and **RM** have slur on n3–4; a slur on n4–5 seems more sensible
	45	Vl. I:	The slur should perhaps be on n2–4, but it looks casually added in **PP**
	59	BC:	In the BM **PP** the flat has been put in by hand; it is possible that not all copies have it
	84	BC:	n1 looks like part of the 'cue', but perhaps it should be played because the part changes to the bass clef before it

119	All:	S has minims on the 3rd beat, and no pause
130		No tempo in Vl. I and B; *Allegro* in other **PP** and in **RM**
132	Vl. II:	n7 B flat in S; BM's **PP** has something inserted by hand which might be a flat.

X   All: **PP**, etc: two-sharp key signature throughout, here adjusted to three sharps. Hence all naturals as for Vl. I 14 n5 are editorial, and all such notes as Vl. I 20 n3 have a sharp in the sources

85	Vl. II:	n3 G natural in **PP** and **RM**; I have presumed an error
110	Vl. II:	n2 D natural in **PP** and **RM**; I have presumed an error
135	Vl. I:	The diagonal line showing where *Piano* starts is given only in Vl. II

XI

8	BC:	Pause on minim in **PP**
15	Vl. I:	n3 D flat in **PP**, which conflicts with BC; **RM** also flattens all the Ds in Vl. I
31	BC:	Figures chaotic through lack of space; I have adjusted them laterally
38	Vl. I:	n8 should perhaps be E natural
66	Vl. I:	n1 should probably be dotted, as also Vl. II's n1 in 67
105	Vl. I:	n5–6 should perhaps be even quavers like the other slurred groups, but they are dotted in **RM** as well as **PP**

XII

1		*Adagio* in **RM** and S; no tempo in **PP** except for Vl. II
1	Vl. II:	n5 A natural in S
98	B:	n5 B flat in S. BM's **PP** has very faint flat which appears to have been put in by hand and then partially erased. Christ Church **PP** has no flat
118	B:	Pause on n2 in **PP**
119ff	All:	**RM** omits every other barline (so that the movement is in our $\frac{6}{8}$) and marks it $\mathrm{C}\!\!\!\!\frac{}{3}\,1$
149	B/BC:	As in **PP**, **RM** and S, but the rhythm should presumably be the same in both parts
161	Vl. I:	As in **PP**, **RM** and S, but Purcell probably meant quaver + crotchet as in 149
179	All:	**RM** has C (unbarred) and no *Adagio*

In all six sonatas **RM** has $\mathrm{C}\!\!\!\!\frac{}{3}\,1$ consistently in three-time movements, virtually no pauses except at the end of each sonata, and all **PP**'s figures over BC together with a good many others.

To the King

May it please yor Maj.^{ty}

I had not assum'd the confidence of laying the following Compositions at your Sacred feet, but that—as they are the immediate Results of your Majesties Royall favour, and benignity to me (which have made me what I am) so, I am constrain'd to hope, I may presume, amongst Others of your Majesties over-oblig'd and altogether underserving Subjects, that your Maj.^{ty} will with your accustom'd Clemency, vouchsafe to Pardon the best Endeavours of

yor Maj.^{ties}

Most Humble and most

Obedient Subject and Servant

H. Purcell

To the Reader

Ingenuous Reader,

Instead of an elaborate harangue on the beauty and the charms of Musick (which after all the learned Encomions that words can contrive commends it Self best by the performances of a skilful hand, and an angelical voice:) I shall Say but a very few things by way of Preface, concerning the following Book, and its Author: for its Author, he has faithfully endeavour'd a just imitation of the most fam'd Italian Masters: principally, to bring the Seriousness and gravity of that Sort of Musick into vogue, and reputation among our Country-men, whose humor, 'tis time now, should begin to loath the levity, and balladry of our neighbours: The attempt he confesses to be bold, and daring, there being Pens and Artists of more eminent abilities, much better qualify'd for the imployment than his, or himself, which he well hopes these weak endeavours will in due time provoke, and enflame to a more acurate undertaking. He is not asham'd to own his unskilfulness in the Italian Language; but that's the unhappiness of his Education, which cannot justly be accounted his fault, however he thinks he may warrantably affirm, that he is not mistaken in the power of the Italian Notes, or elegancy of their Compositions, which he would recommend to the English Artists. There has been neither care, nor industry wanting, as well in contriving, as revising the whole Work; which had been abroad in the world much Sooner, but that he has now thought fit to cause the whole Thorough Bass to be Engraven, which was a thing quite besides his first Resolutions. It remains only that the English Practitioner be enform'd that he will find a few terms of Art perhaps unusual to him, the chief of which are these following: Adagio *and* Grave, *which import nothing but a very slow movement:* Presto Largo, *Poco* Largo, *or* Largo *by it Self, a middle movement:* Allegro, *and* Vivace, *a very brisk, Swift or fast movement:* Piano, *Soft. The Author has no more to add, but his hearty wishes, that his Book may fall into no other hands but theirs who carry Musical Souls about them; for he is willing to flatter himself into a belief, that with Such his labours will Seem neither unpleasant, nor unprofitable.*

Vale

HENRY PURCELL
Zwölf dreistimmige Triosonaten

Die ersten englischen Triosonaten wurden wahrscheinlich um 1620 von Coperario geschrieben. Er hiess eigentlich John Cooper, hatte aber, nachdem er in Italien gewesen war, seinen Namen geändert. Zweifellos, hatte er dort einige der ersten italienischen Sonaten dieser Art zu hören bekommen. Von grösserem Interesse sind die von William Lawes um 1640 geschriebenen Beispiele dieser Musikgattung. Sie bestehen aus drei Sätzen mit den Titeln Fantasia, Alman und Galliard[1], woraus zu ersehen ist, dass sie den früheren, nur für Violen geschriebenen Fantasias und Tänzen, ähnlich waren. So wurde auch in der Tat aus einer dreistimmigen Fantasia für Violen eine Triosonate, wenn ein Tasteninstrument die Basstimme mitspielte. Bei Musik aus jener Zeit lässt es sich oft schwer sagen, ob ein Komponist dabei an die Mitwirkung eines Tasteninstruments gedacht hat, oder nicht. Als Matthew Locke 1656 seinen *Little Consort* herausgab, schien es ihm gleichgültig, auf welche Weise die für ‚zwei Sopranstimmen und eine Basstimme‘ komponierten Suiten gespielt wurden, denn auf dem Titelblatt steht ausdrücklich: ‚Entweder allein, oder mit Theorben und Cembalo zu spielen.‘ Ausserdem schien es ihm auch gleich, ob für die ‚Sopranstimme‘ Violen oder Geigen verwendet wurden.

Ungefähr um diese Zeit komponierte John Jenkins Werke für Kammermusik, die der Triosonate des Barocks in mancher Beziehung näher standen. Sie waren musikalisch gehaltvoller als Lockes *Little Consort* in dem jede Suite aus vier kurzen Sätzen in Tanzform bestand). Auch wurden eindeutig Geigen für den ‚Sopran‘ verlangt, sowie ein Tasteninstrument, das vom Bass aus die Harmonien auszufüllen hatte. Der durchdringendere Ton der Geige war besonders bei den schnelleren Sätzen vonnöten, in denen sich eine gewisse Virtuosität erstmalig bemerkbar machte. Die Entwicklung des Geigenbaus in Italien hatte einen ganz neuen Stil im Spielen ermöglicht, den die Komponisten in ihren Werken zu berücksichtigen begannen. In England wurde jedoch der Gambe (bass viol) weiterhin, und bis nach Purcells Tod, der Vorzug vor dem Cello gegeben, während, was die Tasteninstrumente betraf, die Orgel ebensogut wie das Cembalo herangezogen wurde, denn Kleinorgeln waren in den Wohnungen vieler Leute zu finden. Eine Anzahl der Triosonaten von Jenkins haben sich im Manuskript erhalten, und einige davon sollen 1660 veröffentlicht worden sein. Purcell hat sie gewiss gekannt.

[1] In der *Musica Britannica* XXI, S. 107-126, sind drei von den acht Sonaten, die sich erhalten haben, wiedergegeben, und Beispiele der Kompositionen Coperarios stehen in der *Musica Britannica* IX, S. 183-191.

Purcells Triosonaten unterscheiden sich von denen seiner englischen Vorgänger hauptsächlich auf zweierlei Art: erstens sind sie viel interessanter, und zweitens sind sie im Wesen viel italienischer, besonders in den schnelleren Sätzen. Vor 1683 waren erst wenige italienische Triosonaten gedruckt worden, und es gibt keine Belege dafür, dass Exemplare solcher Ausgaben damals bis nach England gekommen waren. Italienische Musiker kamen jedoch schon nach London, um dort ihren Lebensunterhalt zu verdienen, und es war in solchen Fällen vorgekommen, dass sie handgeschriebene Triosonaten von Komponisten wie Vitali mitgebracht hatten. Ein Manuskript solcher Sonaten im British Museum, Add. 31431, trägt das Datum 1680. Purcell war auf den gesteigert italienischen Charakter seiner eigenen Sonaten stolz, wie er in der Vorrede ,An den Leser' betont hat. Bezeichnenderweise gibt es bei ihm keine Sätze, die den Titel eines Tanzes tragen. Nichtsdestoweniger ist der Einfluss der alten Fantasias doch in einigen Sätzen zu erkennen.

Am 28. Mai 1683 wurde die folgende Ankündigung in der *London Gazette* veröffentlicht: ,Hiermit wird allen den Herren, kundgemacht, die für das von Mr Henry Purcel veröffentlichte Angebot, seine dreistimmigen Sonaten für zwei Geigen und Bass, mit Cembalo oder Orgel zu drucken, subskribiert haben, dass die besagten Bände jetzt ganz fertig sind und ihnen im folgenden Juni, am 11., geliefert werden sollen: ferner jedem, der noch nicht subskribiert hat und noch vor jenem Datum subskribieren will, wie es in dem besagten Angebot steht (welches zehn Schillinge für den ganzen Satz angibt), das in Mr William Halls Haus in der Norfolk Street, oder in Mr Playfords und Mr Carrs Geschäft am Temple zu finden ist; denn die besagten Bände werden nach diesem Datum nicht unter fünfzehn Schillingen der Satz verkauft.' Eine weitere Ankündigung erschien am 11. Juni. Durch sie wurden die Subskribenten aufgefordert, ihre Quittungen zum Hause Purcells in der ,St Anns Lane, auf der anderen Seite der Westminster-Abby' zu bringen, wo sie ,ihre Bände erhalten' würden, nachdem sie den Rest des Geldes bezahlt hätten. Auf dem Titelblatt stand der folgende Text: *Sonnata's in III Stimmen: Zwei Geigen und Bass: Mit Orgel oder Cembalo. Komponiert von Henry Purcell, Ordentlicher Komponist Seiner Hochwürdigen Majestät, und Organist an der Chapell Royall. London, für den Autor gedruckt: und zum Verkauf bei I. Playford und I. Carr am Temple, Fleet Street, 1683.*

Die Subskribenten erhielten nicht drei sondern vier Bände mit den Stimmen für die Instrumente. Sie trugen die Aufschriften Violin Primo, Violin Secundo, Basso und Basso Continuo. Nur der Band mit der ersten Violinstimme enthält das einleitende Material. Es beginnt mit einem Bildnis des Komponisten im Alter von vierundzwanzig Jahren, das R. White gemalt haben soll. Nach dem Titelblatt, dessen Text weiter oben zitiert wurde, steht die Widmung und die Vorrede ‚An den Leser' auf S.XX und S.XXI, dann noch einmal das Titelblatt, und danach die Noten. Jede einzelne Sonate steht in jeder Stimme auf zwei gegenüberliegenden Seiten, und umwenden ist daher unnötig. Verglichen mit späteren Ausgaben, sind die Seiten von kleinem Format.

Kritiker haben sich oft den Kopf zerbrochen, warum Purcell diese Werke ‚Sonnata's of III Parts', und die nach seinem Tode herausgegebenen, ihnen ähnlichen, ‚Sonatas in IV Parts' genannt hat. Aber das ist kein Problem. Für alle Triosonaten werden vier Spieler benötigt, doch gewöhnlich dient eine und dieselbe Stimme für den Gambenspieler und den Spieler des Tasteninstruments. Es kann gut sein, dass Purcells Verleger eine solche Stimme vom Komponisten erwartet hatte und sein Titelblatt in diesem Sinne stechen liess. In der Vorrede ‚An den Leser' steht, dass der Komponist sich diese Frage noch einmal überlegt hatte, doch, wie wir später sehen werden, muss Purcell von jeher vier Bände für seine Stimmen verlangt haben. Als er in diesem Fall darauf bestand, verweigerte Playford die zuzüglichen Kosten für die Korrektur des Titelblatts. Es scheint, dass die Vorrede ‚An den Leser' nicht von Purcell, sondern von Playford geschrieben worden ist.

Die aussergewöhnliche Fehlerlosigkeit der Stimmen zeugt von der Sorgfalt, mit der Purcell das Korrekturlesen vorgenommen hat, und davon spricht er auch in seiner Vorrede ‚An den Leser'. Ein Autographexemplar dieser Sonaten hat sich nicht erhalten, aber selbst wenn eins existierte, würden die gedruckten Stimmen als Quellen den Vorzug verdienen, weil sie das letzte Wort des Komponisten darstellen. Aus diesem Grund folgt der Text der vorliegenden Ausgabe dem der gedruckten Stimmen. Nur an ganz wenigen Stellen weichen die beiden Sätze Stimmen, die für diese Partiturausgabe zum Vergleich herangezogen wurden, voneinander ab, und zwar bei Bindebögen, Vorzeichen und bei der Bezifferung des Basses. Zweifellos liessen sich in anderen Stimmen noch weitere Abweichungen finden. Eine erschöpfende Kollationierung ist nicht vorgenommen worden, doch werden eine Anzahl Abweichungen in den Anmerkungen zum Notentext erwähnt.

Vier handgeschriebene Partituren aus dem siebzehnten Jahrhundert haben sich erhalten. Das schöne Exemplar in der Bibliothek des Christ Church College in Oxford (MS39) trägt alle Anzeichen dafür, dass es von den gedruckten Stimmen abgeschrieben wurde, die sich ebenfalls im Besitz dieser Bibliothek befinden. Es hat daher als Vorlage für diese Ausgabe wenig Wert. In diesem Zusammenhang ist RM MS20.h.9 im British Museum, das von den gedruckten Stimmen in gewissen Einzelheiten abweicht, wesentlich interessanter. Die Worte ‚Im Alter von 25 im Jahre 1683‘, die oben auf der ersten Seite stehen, widersprechen dem heute allgemein akzeptierten Geburtsdatum Purcells. W. H. Cummings besass einmal eine Partitur, von der er annahm, obwohl es nicht stimmte, dass sie von Purcells Hand geschrieben wäre. Auch J. A. Fuller-Maitland, der die Hauptpunkte, in denen die Partitur von den gedruckten Stimmen verschieden war, in seiner Purcell Society Ausgabe aus dem Jahre 1893 anführte, sah sie als Autograph an. Das Manuskript befindet sich jetzt in der Eastman School of Music, Rochester, N.Y. (Sibley 15|1841), und eine weitere Partitur wird im Conservatoire Royal zu Brüssel aufbewahrt MS V. 14. 981).

Die ersten acht Sonaten stehen in Paaren: auf eine Sonate in Moll, folgt jeweils eine in der parallelen Durtonart. Diese Paare schreiten von Tonarten mit Been zu Tonarten mit Kreuzen schrittweise fort. Die letzten vier Sonaten stellen eine Unterbrechung dieser Fortschreitung dar, doch mag es bedeutsam sein, dass die ersten beiden Werke in den späteren *Sonaten in IV Stimmen* in Tonarten stehen, welche diese Fortschreitung fortsetzen könnten, nämlich in H-Moll und Es-Dur. Ursprünglich mag die Sonate in Es-Dur mit der in C-Moll, die als Nr. IX im 1683 gedruckten Stimmensatz steht, ein Paar gebildet haben, und die in H-Moll mit der in D-Dur am Ende. Ausserdem lässt sich aus stilistischen Gründen vermuten, dass die Sonaten in Es-Dur und H-Moll aus der späteren Ausgabe ursprünglich zur früheren gehört haben. Das Adagio zu Beginn der ersteren, wie auch das zweite Adagio der letzteren fängt mit einem Thema wiederholter, punktierter Noten an, wobei die wiederholten Noten eine Quinte über der Tonika stehen. Im späteren Stimmensatz beginnt kein langsamer Satz auf diese Weise, wohl aber eine überraschende Anzahl von

Sätzen in der 1683 veröffentlichen Ausgabe, wie zum Beispiel I 67, V 101, VII 100, VIII 125, X 88 und XI 1; vgl. auch IX 117.

Die anderen Sätze haben ebenfalls verschiedene Eigenschaften gemeinsam. So folgt die Fuge, die ziemlich in der Mitte jeder Sonate steht, besonders dem italienischen Vorbild. Dort, wo sie, wie meist, im geraden Takt geschrieben ist, trägt sie gewöhnlich die Bezeichnung Canzona, und möglicherweise war sie in dem verlorengegangenen Autograph schon immer so bezeichnet worden. Oft gibt es noch einen fugierten Satz gegen Ende der Sonate, und dieser Satz ist dann im Rhythmus tanzartiger als die Canzonen. Zu den fugierten Passagen gehören Umkehrung (XII 105-109) und *Canon per augmentationem* (X 124). Geniale Beispiele des letzteren stehen im Anfangsteil von Nr. VI, einem Kanon in doppelter Verlängerung in der Quinte und der Oktave. Es ist zu bemerken, dass diese fugierten Sätze nicht, wie bei den alten Fantasias eine Reihe von Themen behandeln, sondern sich auf die Melodie, oder die Melodien, des Anfangs beschränken.

Es ist als fast sicher anzunehmen, dass die Noten in der Basso-Continuo-stimme zu Beginn dieser fugierten Sätze, als Hilfsnoten zu deuten sind, die dem Spieler des Tasteninstruments anzeigen, wo er einzusetzen hat. Derartige Passagen sind fast immer in Kurzschrift geschriebene Geigen-stimmen, und sie stehen in der vorliegenden Partitur klein gedruckt (mit vom Herausgeber hinzugefügten Pausen), weil ich der Meinung bin, dass sie nicht gespielt werden sollen. Doch gibt es auch Stellen, an denen durch diese ‚Hilfsnoten' eine kurze, unabhängige Passage für den Bass gegeben wird (III 149, IV 25-6, VII 31-2, IX 83). Die Bedeutung solcher Passagen ist nicht klar. Auch ist es seltsam, dass verschiedentliche dieser ‚Hilfsnoten' beziffert sind.

Bass und Basso-Continuostimme erfreuen sich mitunter einer unge-wöhnlichen Unabhängigkeit (II 1-10, V 129, VI 79-82 und 149-150, IX 3-16 und XI 30). Im *Largo* aus Nr. V sind sie durchweg unabhängig. Vielleicht hat Purcell diesen Satz aus einem vierstimmigen Stück für Streicher entlehnt, und es ist nun die Frage, ob hier ein weiteres Streichinstrument eingesetzt werden sollte, um mit der Basstimme des Tasteninstruments zu spielen. An derartige Passagen muss Purcell in den Fällen gedacht haben, in denen er auf einer separaten Basstimme bestand; ohne eine solche Stimme hätte die Musik keinen Sinn.

ARBEITSWEISE DES HERAUSGEBERS

Ich habe ,Sonnata' (oder,Sonnatta') sowie ,A 3' im Titel eines jeden Werks gestrichen. Es ist nicht nötig gewesen, die von Purcell benutzten Schlüssel zu modernisieren, abgesehen von Schlüsseln für die ,Hilfsnoten' in der Basso-Continuostimme, die grösstenteils Sopranschlüssel waren. Im Bass und in der Basso-Continuostimme habe ich drei kurze Passagen vom Bratschenschlüssel in den Basschlüssel transponiert (V 125-6, IX 91, X 22-3). Purcells Zeitmasse sind, ausser dem $\frac{6}{4}$ in IX 130, unverändert geblieben. Das einzige andere Zeitmass, das nicht dem modernen Gebrauch entspricht, ist $\frac{C}{3}$. Es bedeutet gewöhnlich $\frac{3}{2}$, kann aber auch $\frac{3}{4}$ (XI 69) bedeuten. Ich habe es nicht für nötig gehalten, eine Variante, $\frac{C}{3 1}$, die manchmal in einer der vier Stimmen, aber nie in mehr als zwei Stimmen steht, besonders anzuführen. Purcells doppelte Taktstriche sind ohne weiteres beibehalten worden. Die, welche in der Mitte eines Satzes stehen, sind als Wiederholungszeichen anzusehen (VI 109). Dort, wo sich das Tempo oder die Dynamik innerhalb eines Taktes ändert, hat Purcell das gewöhnlich durch einen diagonalen Strich in einer der Stimmen angegeben, um genau zu zeigen, wo diese Änderung vorzunehmen ist (I 79 und X 135). Auch diese Striche sind ohne weiteres beibehalten worden. Gebundene halbe Noten habe ich zu ganzen gemacht, und die Schreibart der Bindungen, die über den Taktstrich hinausgehen, habe ich modernisiert. Alle Hinweise des Herausgebers (es sind nur wenige) stehen in Klammern; ausgenommen sind hinzugefügte Bindebögen, die durch einen senkrechten Strich in der Mitte des Bogens gekennzeichnet sind. Alle vom Herausgeber hinzugefügten Bindebögen sind durch authentische Bögen in ähnlichen Passagen an anderen Stellen gerechtfertigt.

Pausenzeichen am Ende der Sätze sind verblüffend uneinheitlich. Man möchte meinen, Purcell hätte nur über dem obersten Liniensystem eine Pause geschrieben, die sein Kupferstecher zuweilen vergessen hat, den tieferen Stimmen beizufügen; doch hat die erste Geigenstimme gar keine Pausenzeichen, ausser in VII 113, sowie im letzten Takt einer jeden Sonate. Sie ist sogar in vielen Fällen die einzige Stimme, die keine Pausen hat. Vielleicht waren diese Pausen dazu da, um den Spielern der tieferen Stimmen anzuzeigen, dass sie auf den ersten Geiger aufpassen sollten, um einen reinen Einsatz im nächsten Teil des Satzes zu erzielen. Wo nur eine Stimme eine Pause hat, habe ich sie als ein Irrtum angesehen und sie lediglich in den Anmerkungen zum Notentext vermerkt. Wo Pausen in mindestens zwei Stimmen stehen, habe ich sie den restlichen Stimmen beigefügt.

Purcell hat kaum je, wie wir es tun, von vornherein angenommen, dass ein Vorzeichen im selben Takt auch später für die gleiche Note gilt. Wenn er das Vorzeichen nicht wiederholt hat, so hat er es nur darum nicht getan, weil er kein Vorzeichen wollte. Wie alle Komponisten seiner Zeit, machte er die im Anfang vorgeschriebenen Vorzeichen nicht mit unserem Auflösungszeichen, sondern mit einem Kreuz oder einem ♭ ungültig. So schrieb er in I 42, Vl.I:

Ohne Kreuz würde man annehmen, dass die fünfte Note ein Es ist. Ich habe Purcells Vorzeichen modernisiert und sie dort gestrichen, wo sie heute überflüssig scheinen, während ich jene, die ein Musiker heutzutage erwarten würde, in Klammern hinzugefügt habe (z.B. II 10, Basso). Es muss ausdrücklich betont werden, dass Auflösungszeichen, die in Klammern stehen, nicht einem Einfall des Herausgebers zu verdanken sind sondern anzeigen, was von Purcell ganz bestimmt beabsichtigt war. Jeder, der es für nötig hält, kann Purcells eigene Vorzeichen von dem ableiten, was weiter oben gesagt worden ist.

Weiterhin habe ich die überflüssigen Vorzeichen in Purcells Tonartvorzeichnung entfernt, wie aus dem weiter oben angeführten Notenbeispiel ersichtlich ist. Ich habe seine Tonartvorzeichnung mit zwei ♭ für die Sonate IX in C-Moll stehen lassen, sowie die Vorzeichnung mit drei ♭ für die Sonate XI in F-Moll, weil es nicht nur in Purcells sondern auch in Händels Zeiten gebräuchlich war, diese Tonarten so zu schreiben. Jedoch auf die Gefahr hin, inkonsequent zu erscheinen, habe ich die Tonartvorzeichnung der Sonate X in A-Dur berichtigt, denn Purcells Schreibart war hier durch seine Zeit bedingt und würde heute nur irreführen. Diese Änderung hatte eine ganze Anzahl von Berichtigungen im bezifferten Bass zur Folge. Auch in diesem Falle wurden die Vorzeichen mit dem modernen Gebrauch in Übereinstimmung gebracht. Es wird auffallen, dass Purcell dort, wo zwei Zahlen für einen Akkord stehen, die tiefere Zahl über die höhere gesetzt hat. Der Zweck, den er damit verfolgt hat, ist gewöhnlich aus den Geigenstimmen ersichtlich.

Roger Fiske, 1974

An den Leser

Geistvoller Leser,

Anstatt einer umständlichen Ansprache über Schönheit und Reiz der Musik (welche sich schliesslich, nach allen gelehrten Lobreden, die aus Worten gedrechselt werden können, am besten selbst durch eine geübte Hand und eine Engelsstimme empfiehlt), will ich nur sehr weniges in einer Vorrede sagen, die sich auf das folgende Buch und seinen Autor bezieht. Was den Autor anbelangt, so hat er sich ernstlich bemüht, die berühmtesten italienischen Meister nachzuahmen; vor allem, um dem Ernst und der Bedeutsamkeit dieser Art von Musik zu Beliebtheit und gutem Ruf unter unseren Landsleuten zu verhelfen, denn es wird Zeit, dass sie in ihren Sinnen danach trachten, anzufangen, die Frivolität und Balladerei unserer Nachbarn zu verabscheuen: ein kühner, waghalsiger Versuch, gibt er zu, denn es gibt bedeutend fähigere Leute, deren Feder und Kunst dazu viel eher taugen als seine Talente, oder er selbst, weshalb er erbstlich hofft, dass diese ärmlichen Versuche sie dereinst zu einem richtigeren Unternehmen anspornen und begeistern werden. Er schämt sich nicht seiner Ungeschicklichkeit in der italienischen Sprache, denn das liegt an seiner traurigen Erziehung, für die er gerechterweise nicht verantwortlich gemacht werden kann, doch meint er, versichern zu können, dass er sich nicht in der Kraft italienischer Noten täuscht, noch in der Eleganz italienischer Kompositionen, welche er den englischen Künstlern empfehlen möchte. Weder Sorgfalt noch Fleiss sind gespart worden bei der

Gestaltung und Revision des ganzen Werks, welches seinen Weg in die Welt viel eher gemacht, wenn es dem Autor jetzt nicht recht gedünkt hätte, den ganzen Generalbass stechen zu lassen, was ein ganz andres Ding war, als was er zunächst beschlossen. Es muss nur noch gesagt werden, um den englischen Ausübenden darüber zu unterrichten, dass er wohl einige künstlerische Bezeichnungen finden wird, die ihm ungewöhnlich erscheinen mögen, worunter die häuptsachlichsten die folgenden sind: Adagio *und* Grave, *die nichts andres bedeuten, als dass der Satz sehr langsam ist:* Presto Largo, Poco Largo *oder* Largo *allein bedeuten einen mittleren Satz:* Allegro *und* Vivace *einen sehr lebhaften, raschen oder schnellen Satz:* Piano, Leise. *Weiteres hat der Autor nicht hinzuzufügen, als seine herzlichen Wünsche, dass dieses Buch nur in die Hände derer fallen mag, die musikalische Seelen in sich tragen; denn er möchte sich selbst in dem Glauben schmeicheln, dass bei solchen Leuten seine Werke weder als unerfreulich noch unvorteilhaft angesehen werden.*

V a l e

Deutsche Übersetzung Stefan de Haan

Twelve Sonatas of Three Parts

VII

Henry Purcell
(1659–1695)

VIII

Violin I

Violin II

Basso

Basso
Continuo

IX

X

26

EE 6636

29

EE 6636

30

EE 6636

XI

32

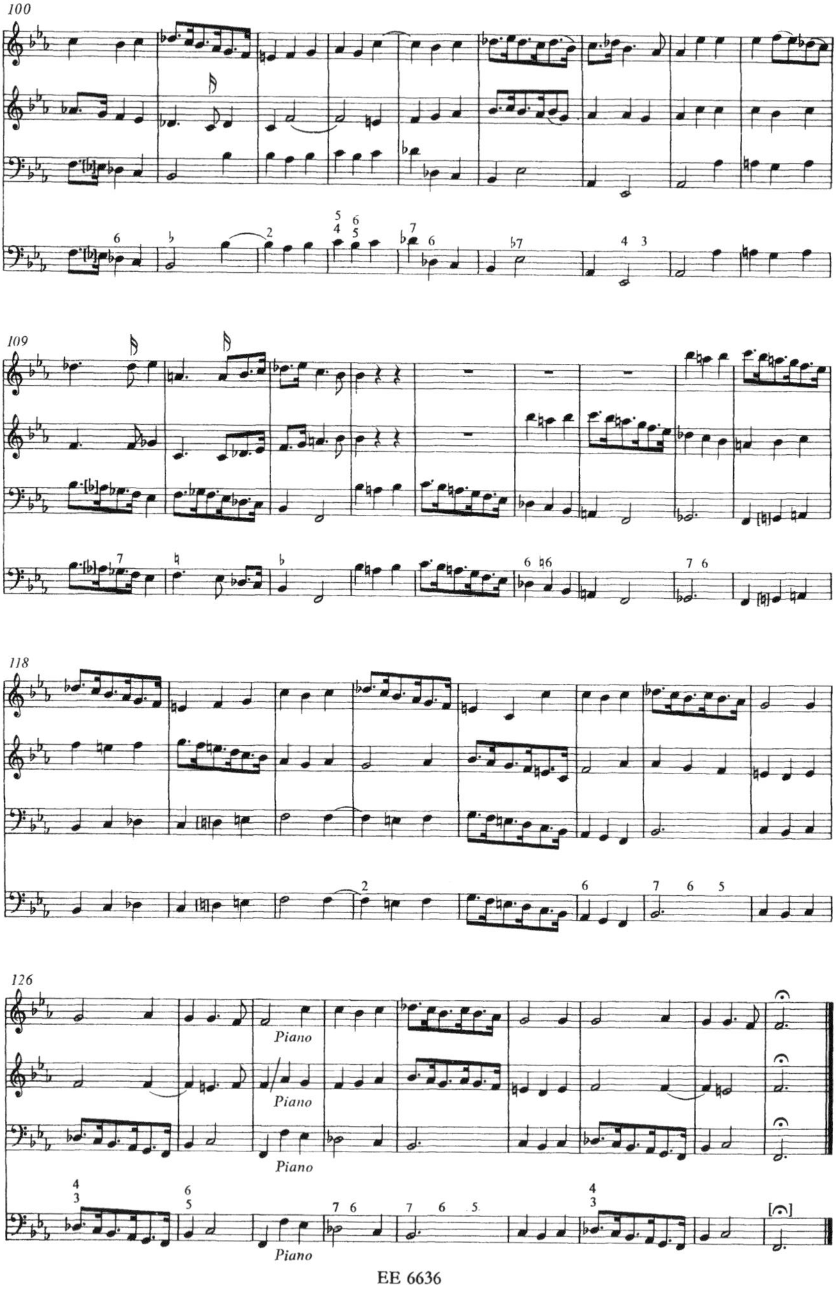
100
109
118
126
Piano
Piano
Piano
Piano

XII

38